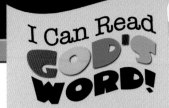

I Can Read
GOD'S
WORD!

Treasure in Heaven
and other stories Jesus told

BARBOUR
PUBLISHING

PHIL A. SMOUSE

In him was life,
and that life was the light of men.

John 1:4 NIV

Published by Barbour Publishing, Inc., P.O. Box 719, Uhrichsville, Ohio 44683
www.barbourbooks.com

Our mission is to publish and distribute inspirational products offering exceptional value and biblical encouragement to the masses.

 Member of the
Evangelical Christian
Publishers Association

Printed in China.
5 4 3 2

CONTENTS

A NOTE TO PARENTS. . .

I Can Read God's Word! is a simple idea with a simple goal: to put the Word of God on the lips of God's children.

I've drawn from the practical teachings of Jesus in the New Testament and the promises of God in the Old and "translated" them into an easy-to-read paraphrase that is absolutely faithful to the original text while staying as close as possible to the phonics-based reading curriculum your children are learning at home or in school.

Twenty-three long years went by before I ever read a single page of the Bible for myself. But if God answers prayer (and you know He does), before *this* year is over you will hear a familiar little voice say, "Mom, Dad, listen. . .*I Can Read God's Word!*"

Enjoy!

Phil A. Smouse

THE LAMP

Jesus said,
"When you light a lamp
what do you do with it?"

"Do you hide it
in a bowl?"

"Do you put it under the bed?"

"No. You set it on a stand!"

"Then everyone
can see the light."

"Are you hiding
God's Word
deep down
in your heart?"

"Let it out!"

"Shine your light
so everyone can see!"

MY TREASURE

Matthew 6:19-21

Jesus said,
"Do not store up
treasure for yourself
in this life."

"That kind of treasure
can be lost for good."

"Or a thief may take it all away."

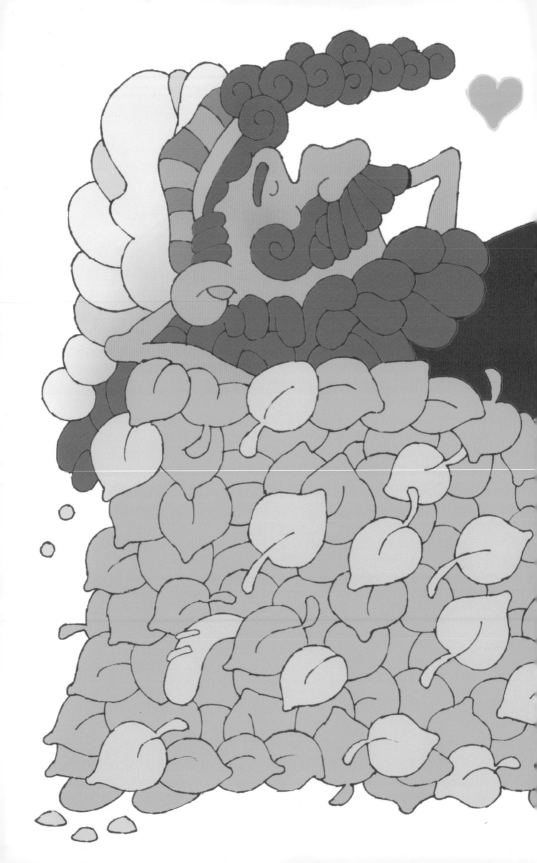

"So store up your treasure
with God in heaven."

"There it cannot be lost."

"And no one
can take it away."

"For the place you hide
your treasure is the
same place your *heart*
will be kept."

ON THE ROCK

Matthew 7:24-27

Jesus said,
"If you hear my words,
then do what I say.
You will be like a wise
man who built his
house on a rock."

"The rain came down."

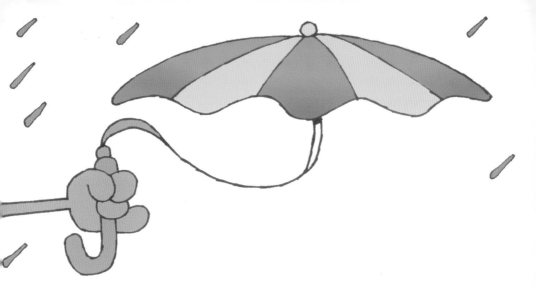

"The floodwater rose."

"A mighty wind
beat against his house."

"But his house did not fall!
It was built tall and strong
on the rock of God's Word."

"But if you hear my words and do not do what I say, you are like a foolish man who built his house on sand."

"The rain came down.
The floodwater rose.
A mighty wind beat
against his house."

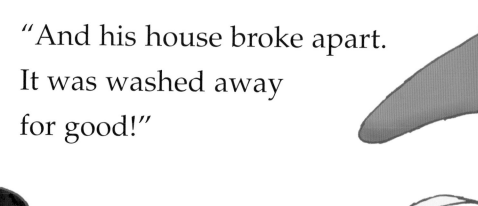

"And his house broke apart.
It was washed away
for good!"

Jesus said,

"Love your enemy."

"If he hurts you,
pray for him."

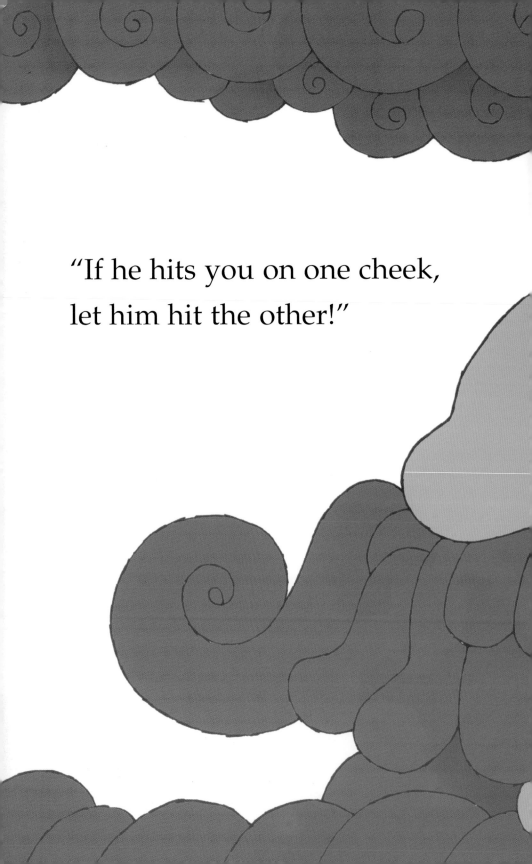

"If he hits you on one cheek,
let him hit the other!"

"If he takes your coat,
do not stop him."

"Give him your shirt!"

"Whatever you
want him to
do to you. . ."

"You do that to him!"

THE LAMP   Luke 8:16–17

"No one, when he has lit a lamp, covers it with a vessel or puts it under a bed, but sets it on a lampstand, that those who enter may see the light. For nothing is secret that will not be revealed, nor anything hidden that will not be known and come to light."

MY TREASURE   Matthew 6:19–21

"Do not lay up for yourselves treasures on earth, where moth and rust destroy and where thieves break in and steal; but lay up for yourselves treasures in heaven, where neither moth nor rust destroys and where thieves do not break in and steal. For where your treasure is, there your heart will be also."

ON THE ROCK   Matthew 7:24–27

"Therefore whoever hears these sayings of Mine, and does them, I will liken him to a wise man who built his house on the rock: and the rain descended, the floods came, and the winds blew and beat on that house; and it did not fall, for it was founded on the rock. But everyone who hears these sayings of Mine, and does not do them, will be like a foolish man who built his house on the sand: and the rain descended, the floods came, and the winds blew and beat on that house; and it fell. And great was its fall."

LOVE YOUR ENEMY   Luke 6:27–31

"Love your enemies, do good to those who hate you, bless those who curse you, and pray for those who spitefully use you. To him who strikes you on the one cheek, offer the other also. And from him who takes away your cloak, do not withhold your tunic either. Give to everyone who asks of you. And from him who takes away your goods do not ask them back. And just as you want men to do to you, you also do to them likewise."